JOE MAUER
Baseball Superstar

BY ANTHONY WACHOLTZ

CAPSTONE PRESS
a capstone imprint

Sports Illustrated KIDS Superstar Athletes is published by Capstone Press,
1710 Roe Crest Drive, North Mankato, Minnesota 56003.
www.capstonepub.com

Books published by Capstone Press are manufactured with paper
containing at least 10 percent post-consumer waste.

Library of Congress Cataloging-in-Publication Data
Wacholtz, Anthony.
    Joe Mauer : baseball superstar / by Anthony Wacholtz.
    p. cm.—(Sports illustrated kids. Superstar Athletes.)
    Summary: "Presents the athletic biography of Joe Mauer, including his career as a high school
and professional baseball player"—Provided by publisher.
    ISBN 978-1-4296-7683-0 (library binding)
    ISBN 978-1-4296-8003-5 (paperback)
    1. Mauer, Joe, 1983– —Juvenile literature. 2. Baseball players—United States—
Biography—Juvenile literature. I. Title. II. Series.
GV865.M376W33 2012
796.357092—dc23
[B]   2011028689

Editorial Credits
Aaron Sautter, editor; Ted Williams, designer; Eric Gohl, media researcher;
    Laura Manthe, production specialist

Photo Credits
Newscom/Icon SMI 700/Vince Muzik, 9; KRT/Joe Oden, 10; RTR/Eric Miller, 7
Sports Illustrated/Al Tielemans, 1, 15, 22 (all), 23, 24; Damian Strohmeyer,
    cover (all), 2–3, 21; David E. Klutho, 19; John Biever, 5, 13, 14, 16

Design Elements
Shutterstock/chudo-yudo, designerpix, Fassver Anna, Fazakas Mihaly

Direct Quotations
Pages 11 and 20, from www.367sports.com/baseball/mlb/quotes/Joe_mauer.php

Printed in the United States of America in North Mankato, Minnesota.

102011   006405CGS12

TABLE OF CONTENTS

CHAPTER 1

MAUER POWER

On October 1, 2006, the Minnesota Twins battled the Chicago White Sox for the division title. The two teams were trying to win the American League (AL) Central division.

Twins catcher Joe Mauer also had another race in mind. He led the league with a .346 **batting average**. But Derek Jeter of the New York Yankees was only one point behind him. The Yankees were playing the Toronto Blue Jays that same day.

batting average—a measure of how often a player gets a hit

The Twins were down 1-0 early in the game. But they came back to win 5-1. The team won the AL Central division. Mauer had two hits in four **at bats**. His average climbed to .347.

Jeter had only one hit in five at bats against the Blue Jays. He ended with a .343 average. Mauer won the 2006 batting title. He became the first catcher to lead the majors in batting average.

at bat—when a batter faces a pitcher and tries to hit the ball

Joe Mauer celebrates winning the 2006 AL Central Division title with Twins fans

CHAPTER 2

HOMETOWN HERO

Joseph Patrick Mauer was born in St. Paul, Minnesota. He played basketball, football, and baseball at Cretin-Derham Hall high school. As the starting quarterback, he led the football team to a state title in 1999. He had even more success in baseball. His batting average was over .500 each season. He struck out only once in four years.

Florida State University offered Mauer a **scholarship** to play football. But he entered the 2001 Major League Baseball (MLB) **draft** instead. The Minnesota Twins picked him first overall. He was the first catcher in 16 years to be the number one pick.

"It was always baseball for me. This is what I always wanted to do." — Joe Mauer

scholarship—money given to a student to pay for school
draft—the process of choosing a person to join a sports team

CHAPTER 3

HITTING THE MAJORS

Mauer played two years in the **minor leagues**. He entered the majors in 2004. But after only two games, Mauer hurt his knee chasing a foul ball. He returned a month later, but still had knee problems. The Twins wanted to be careful with their rookie catcher. They kept him off the field the rest of the season.

minor league—a league of teams where players improve their playing skills before joining a major league team

Mauer bounced back in 2005. He played the entire season. Then he really hit his stride in 2006. He pounded out 181 hits, 13 home runs, and 84 RBIs. His hitting and great defensive play led to his first All-Star Game that year.

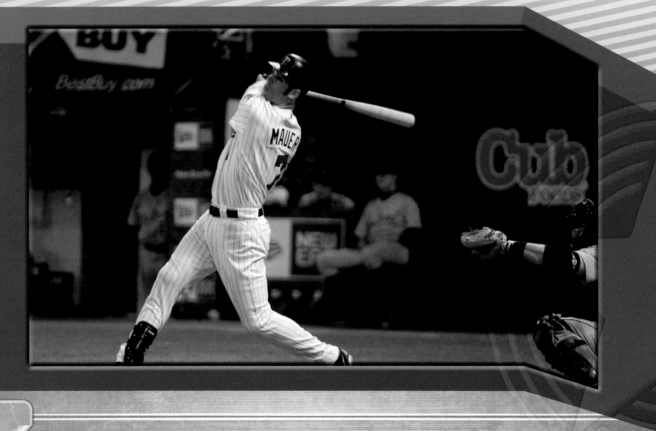

MR. SIDEBURNS

Joe Mauer is known for powerful hitting, tough defense—and his sideburns! The star catcher is famous for his long sideburns. Mauer's biggest fans even wear fake sideburns while watching him play.

Mauer's hitting dropped a little in 2007. But he returned to his great play in 2008. His .328 average led the American League. It also led to his second All-Star Game.

Mauer had an even better season in 2009. He hit .365 to win his third batting title. He also smashed 28 home runs and 96 RBIs. And he made a third trip to the All-Star Game. Mauer's amazing play earned him the 2009 AL Most Valuable Player (MVP) award.

Mauer was smashing the ball, but Twins fans were worried. His **contract** lasted only through the 2010 season. Other teams were interested in the All-Star catcher. But the Twins wanted to keep their hometown hero. Mauer signed an eight-year contract with the Twins in March 2010.

contract—a legal agreement

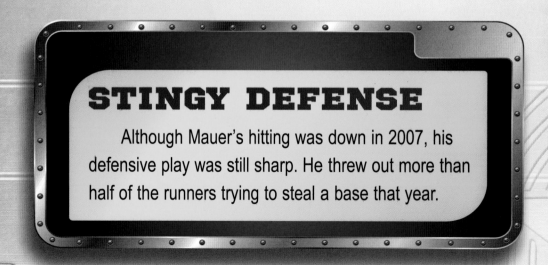

STINGY DEFENSE

Although Mauer's hitting was down in 2007, his defensive play was still sharp. He threw out more than half of the runners trying to steal a base that year.

CHAPTER 4

HARD WORK AND SUCCESS

Joe Mauer is one of the best players in baseball. He works hard to improve every part of his game. The slugger is a proven leader who drives his teammates to succeed. Baseball fans have a lot to cheer for with Mauer behind the plate.

"I'm looking to get better, and anything that will help me accomplish that, I'm all ears." — Joe Mauer

INTERNET SITES

FactHound offers a safe, fun way to find Internet sites related to this book. All of the sites on FactHound have been researched by our staff.

Here's all you do:

Visit *www.facthound.com*

Type in this code: 9781429676830

 Check out projects, games and lots more at **www.capstonekids.com**

INDEX